There was a young fellow called Glover
Who bowled fifteen wides in an over,
Which had never been done
By a clergyman's son
On a Sunday, in August, at Dover.

There was a young fellow called Glover . . .
Sporting Limericks

Edited by Simon Barnes
With illustrations by Tim Jaques

The Kingswood Press

Also by Simon Barnes:
Phil Edmonds – A Singular Man

The Kingswood Press
an imprint of William Heinemann Ltd
10 Upper Grosvenor Street, London W1X 9PA

LONDON MELBOURNE
JOHANNESBURG AUCKLAND

First published 1987

0 434 98121 4

Typeset by Rowland Phototypesetting Ltd,
Bury St Edmunds, Suffolk
Printed and bound in Great Britain by
Redwood Burn Ltd, Trowbridge

The editor and publisher would like to extend their appreciation to Times Newspapers Limited, Annalise Kay, Beryl Hill, Sophie Reeves, Chris Perring, Simon Daffarn, and especially to Leo Cooper.

Special thanks are due to all those who submitted limericks, whether or not they have been included.

A sportsman who takes second place,
Should be able to say with good grace:
    'It is true, don't you see
    He played better than me,'
And still have a smile on his face.

J. S. MEYRICK

For clean British fun, just the ticket,
On table or fairway or wicket,
    The Englishman's ball
    Is the roundest of all,
So WHACK it, or THWACK it, or KICK it!

ALAN CLARK

A member of parliament brings,
To archery statesmanlike things,
  And scores any bulls
  Not by strings that he pulls
But rather by pulling the strings.
R. G. PRINGLE

An archer called Norman le Beau
Scored gold after gold in a reau.
  When asked to explain
  His success, he was vain:
'I'm simply the best, don't you kneau?'
D. A. H. BYATT

At Plymouth, Drake bowled on the hoe
He said 'I'm left-handed you know'.
　　His sinister woods
　　Delivered the goods
As he cackhandedly finished the foe.
MIKE BARNARD

A Badminton player from Nuthall,
Bred poultry and wove cloth – most subtle.
    But a mental contusion
    Led him into confusion
Now he can't tell a cock from a shuttle!
F. G. ROBINSON

A Scot with considerable labour
Grew adept at tossing the caber:
    From his garden one day
    It went sailing away
And flattened his lawn-mowing neighbour.

MRS ALISON MORGAN

Henry Cooper, a boxer of late,
Has met a remarkable fate;
    He was asked by M. Thatcher
    To be a vote-catcher
And now he's the new head of state.
                JILLIAN GRIFFITHS

There is a spin bowler called Emburey,
Whose spin-bowling partner is Edmonds,
    He tosses them up
    And gets lots of wickets
But sometimes gets hit for six in the process.
              SUSAN RICHARDSON

An eighty-year-old geriatric,
Played cricket one day at Kilpatrick;
    He knocked up a score
    Of a hundred and four
And ended the game with a hat trick.
               R. EDGEWORTH JOHNSTONE

A brilliant young cricketer, Botham,
Said, 'Reporters? I hate 'em, I loathe 'em:
    They should not mount attacks
    Without checking their facts
As my forthcoming court case will show them!'
               MEG BUXTON

A young test team captain named Gower,
Wished the West Indies side would bowl slower.
    Said he, 'There's no peace
    When we're in at the crease
And a minute seems more like an hour.

'It's no wonder my lads fail to stick it,
For what's played over here isn't cricket.
    The fast life's all right
    When we're out for the night
But not when we're out at the wicket.'

SYD HOLTAM

There was a young fellow from Dover,
Who with women was no Casanova.
    So taking up cricket
    He aimed at the wicket
And soon bowled a good maiden over.
PHYLLIS HARTNOLL

There was a young batsman of Kent,
Whose career showed a startling ascent,
    Till an umpire I know
    Used a straight edge to show
That his bat was unlawfully bent.
J. L. RICE

D. I. Gower was standing on seven,
When 'Out' (l.b.w.) was given.
    Just before he was hit
    He had finished the bit
That comes before – 'Which art in Heaven'.
                    J. NISBET

A cricketer, bowling for Sarum,
Said: 'Them wot 'ave pads better warum –
    But warum instead
    Not on legs but their 'ead,
'Cos I aims not to bowl 'em but scarum!'
             DONALD CHRISTIE

15

A devilish bowler called Garner,
Swerves balls like a lethal banana;
    They zip up and down
    Crushing toe, cracking crown
Nipping flesh like a hungry piranha.
                    EDWARD CAST

There once was a man from Nepal,
Who went to a fancy dress ball.
 He bought gloves and pads;
 It was one of his fads
As he never played cricket at all.
MRS H. GRIFFIN AND MANY OTHERS

A foolish young batsman named Wally,
When hit on the toe, shouted 'Golly!'
 If he'd only cried 'God!'
 Or 'Blast you, you sod!'
He'd be praised, not sent home for his folly.
    E. PICKARD

A happy spectator told Gower:
'It's de diet dey eats give dem power;
  De bananas give twist
  To de turn of de wrist
And de rum make dem burst into flower!'
M. LATTIN

Ian Botham, attempting to flick it
For six, made a gift of his wicket.
    Said Gower, 'It's fun
    To hit a home run
But you do it in baseball, not cricket'.
                    NORMAN HAMMOND

There was a young man who played cricket,
Who performed well in front of the wicket.
    When caught OUT at last
    He said, 'Not so fast
Or my union will call out a picket'.
                        M. I. BIGGS

At cricket the Windies have won,
Coming down on our chaps like a ton,
    But the shouting and riot
    Puts a note of disquiet
In a game that used to be fun.
JONATHAN BOOTH

When they beat the Australians, Gower
And his team were the men of the hour;
    But their current demise
    Provokes only cries
Of 'What an incompetent shower!'
PHILIP NICHOLSON

Our cricketers out in the sun,
Appear to be having great fun –
    Oh I know I'm a nagger,
    But drinks with Mick Jagger
When we're losing, it just isn't done.
              BRIDGET NEWBOLT

There was a young fellow named Gatting,
World famous for pugnacious batting,
    His whites are a sight;
    They're always so tight:
They're straining to hold all his fat in.
              NICK BRYANT

Cried the bowler: 'My pitch has been queered –
The target has quite disappeared;
    There stands W. G. Grace
    With a grin on his face,
And I can't see the stumps for his beard!'
              JOHN DINAN

There was a great batsman from Surrey,
Who one day ate huge plates of curry.
    Next day at the Test
    He was not at his best
But he got lots of runs in a hurry!

                  ELAINE M. COOPER

When West Indies out-bat all our bowlers,
And our batsmen all fear for their molars,
    It's really a shame
    They're eluded by fame:
What they need is to clone a few Zolas.

                  ROBERT WADDINGTON

Said the Reverend Shepherd to May,
'My dear Peter, you've got all the say;
Test committee's selection
Needs higher reflection
And I have the Lord's ear every day.'
VICTOR BALHAM

'I'm sick of this game,' Gatting said.
'They keep chucking the ball at my head.
    What's the use of a bat
    If they aim at my hat?
They should give me a racquet instead!'
REG HORSFIELD

A striker said, passing the picket:
'Don't black me – I'm off to play cricket.
    Industrial action
    Wins this satisfaction:
The right to strike, white, at the wicket!'
DONALD CHRISTIE

Gooch, Gower, Both, Gatting and Lamb
Made the Aussies seem 'money for jam';
    But fast bowling riches
    On dubious pitches
Have revealed the extent of the sham.
                  RICHARD WATTS

Antiguans like Viv should be crowned,
For the joy that they spread all around;
    But silly old birds
    With provocative words
Should be tied up with barbed wire, and drowned.
                  JOHN HUME

Half-asleep in the shade of the trees,
Eyes closed, and fanned by the breeze,
    I hear from my pillow
    Leather on willow
And the taking of afternoon teas.
DAVID CRAM

In Kingston a fella called Gatting,
Had his nose badly broken while batting;
    He said 'It's like war,
    The pitch is so poor:
It wouldn't have happened on matting!'
JOHN HOOK

There at the wicket stood Borrow,
His face white with anger, not sorrow.
　　He gave a great shout
　　'That was never out!'
'Oh no? Read the paper tomorrow!'
　　　　　　COLIN GREENWOOD

If the dartboard is not to be missed,
Several pints of strong ale might assist.
    Those who've mastered the art
    Of throwing a dart
Bend the elbow as much as the wrist.

NICK ALLOWAY

A punter from county Kildare,
Grew rich at the dogs (which is rare).
    When asked how it's done
    He replied, 'Just for fun,
I bet ten pounds "win" on the hare'.
                                    ROSE MITRE

There was a young punter called Bertie,
Who said to his pa, 'Don't be shirty.
    You know times are lean
    And I lost every bean
When I put my shirt on the two-thirty!'
                            MARGARET PEARSON

A fencing instructor named Fiske
Had movements so terribly brisk
That the speed of his action
And the Fitzgerald Contraction
Foreshortened his foil to a disc.
SUBMITTED BY B. COOK

The Fitzgerald Contraction is a consequence of Einstein's Theory of Relativity, in that as the speed of an object approaches that of light, its length decreases, until at the speed of light it would have no length at all.

A soccer star narrowly missed
The goal, and was grieved to be hissed.
    So he broke down in tears
     To ironic cheers
'Cos he'd hoped to be cuddled and kissed.
JOSEPH D. KNIGHT

A Millwall supporter named Joe,
Was attacked by five boot-boys from Bow;
 He drew a last breath
 And intoned at his death:
'Here we go, here we go, here we go . . .'
      JOHN DINAN

A player of football named Blissett,
Would shoot for the goal, and yet miss it.
 Causing fans of his team
 To excitedly scream
That his presence on Earth was illicit.
      OSCAR DAVIES

Soccer, that terrible bore,
Really needn't be played anymore;
    Our concern is the pools
    Not the skill or the rules
So to hell with the game; what's the score?
BILL EVANS

To cope with the hoodlums and yobs,
Armed with murderous thingumibobs,
    Let us bring back the 'cat' –
    It's as simple as that:
We must lead, and not follow, the mobs.
RICHARD WATTS

An Arsenal groupie called May,
Who'd been with them to Leeds for the day,
Said, 'I cannot recall,
If I had one or all,
But I know that I had it away'.

ELIZABETH FENWICK

A renegade newsman named Cort,
Tried his hand at cub-shooting – for sport.
    Like a flash from her den
    Shot the vixen – Amen.
(He'll have no further news to report.)
                H. TEMPLE PATTERSON

Said a man: 'Gee, this soccer match shatters,
An illusion I've held re. it's status;
    Why, just kicking the ball
    Doesn't matter at all –
It's the kick in the groin that most matters!'
              PASCOE POLGLAZE

There was a young golfer from Sheen,
Who found, when he got on the green,
    That a renegade mole
    Had dug a large hole
On his line where his putt would have been.
J. L. RICE

A golfer who reached for his driver,
Was felled by a wayward skydiver.
    It's sad to be said
    But both sportsmen are dead.
So farewell from their fans. Where's my fiver?
NICK ALLOWAY

A trendy young golfer called Deans
Had a bad case of 'yips' on the greens,
But it wasn't his putter
That caused him to stutter,
But the tees in his ultra tight jeans.
MICHAEL CLAUGHTON

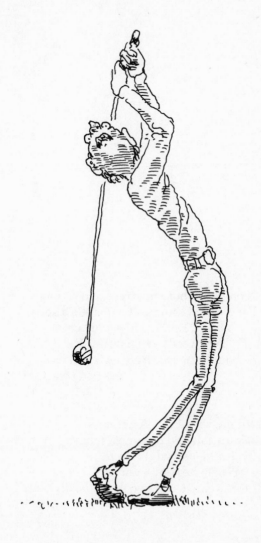

A banker whose mistress had sighed,
For a gift of some golf clubs she'd spied,
    Didn't hear his love mutter
    'Two woods and a putter,'
So bought her St. Andrew's and Ryde.
                            BASIL GARLAND

A yuppy with First Asiatic,
Took up golf and became a fanatic;
    But he played the M.D.
    Whom he beat 4 and 3,
Now his card's marked as upwardly static.
                            E. J. PAWSEY

Yelled a jockey at Epsom racecourse,
As he galloped with hurricane force,
　　'I've beaten the lot!'
　　But the crowd cried, 'You clot!
Go back! You've forgotten your horse!'
FRANK RICHARDS
(SUBMITTED BY SUSAN CONNOR)

An equestrian rider named Morse,
Fell madly in love with his horse;
 Said his wife, 'You rapscallion,
 That horse is a stallion.
This constitutes grounds for divorce.'
VICTOR BALHAM

ON YOUR MARKS! What possessed me? Dunno!
Where's Jeanette? Bloody rain! Told her so!
    Now then! SET! Holy cow!
    Need a pee! Too late now!
Handkerchief? Where the hell did I . . . GO!
DAVID CRAM

'I *love* polo' cried Gigi du Pre,
So Tom straddled a large fallen tree;
   He whacked like a champ
    With his neatly furled gamp –
'Non, ze *mint*, not ze game, mon cheri'.
JANE STEEL-JESSOP

It's unwise to lay bets on the races,
Whether Flat, or in winter, the 'Chases:
    For you'll find it will hurt
    Losing not just your shirt,
But your trousers, your belt and your braces.
J. M. GRANT

She'd streaked across Wembley and Twickers,
Distracting the most hardened kickers;
    But her end was quite grisly:
    She tried it at Bisley,
Forgetting her bullet-proof knickers.

DAVID LILLEY

There was a young stand-off from Neath,
Who habitually played in false teeth.
    When dropping a goal
    He swallowed them whole;
His opponents are sending the wreath.

                    ANON

The coach of a XV at Twickenham,
Had a lot of trouble in picking 'em;
    He said to his Board
    'I'll sort out this horde –
I'll roughen and toughen and thicken 'em'.

                GILBERT GEARY

A Swansea prop forward called Keith
Gradually lost all his teeth;
    So now in the scrums
    He uses his gums
To gnash his opponents from Neath.
           JAMES THOM

A concourse of elderly vicars,
Went off to watch rugby at Twickers.
    They agreed, in their day
    There was far better play
And the chaps all wore much longer knickers.
           ELIZABETH HARDY

Did you hear that my rugger-mad chum,
Got terribly mauled in the scrum?
    His left ear, I fear,
    Finished up in the beer
And his teeth in the Number Eight's bum.

J. L. WILSON

61

A rugby-mad maiden named Sue
Was awarded her 'varsity Blue.
    When I asked this fair maid
    What position she played
'I'm their hooker,' she smiled – which was true.
                    JOHN DINAN

In rugby the rules of decorum
Reap results – and you mustn't ignore 'em! –
    For though drop-kicks and tries
    Gain the points that we prize,
It's the penalty kicks that out-score 'em!
                    JOHN DINAN

A rugby reporter from France,
Said: 'In Wales there's an air of romance.
    Their crowds are so pally,
    They even cry – 'Allez!
Warateg mes amis et bonne chance!'

    * 'Warateg' = Welsh, for 'Play the game!'
             NOEL A. JONES

My uncle Hieronymus Kale,
Wore his bowler when out for a sail:
   'It protects me,' he said
   'When the boom strikes my head,
And it's useful if one needs to bail.'
B. R. DAVIS

An oarsman of Oxford defected,
To Cambridge, but wasn't selected,
    So he pulled some bold strokes
    With those KGB blokes,
Now he rows where he wants, undetected.

TIM SHEET

After losing a decade to Ox,
Light blues with their hearts in their socks,
   Discovered the value
   In using a gal: you
Diminish the weight of your cox.
JOHN MOORE

A pedantic young marksman named Potter
Winged an old lady – the rotter!
    When asked for his reason
    Laughed, 'Well, it's the season
And she said she was game so I shot 'er'.

BILLIE M. PEARCE

At St. Moritz, we've noticed the males,
Dress for skiing in toppers and tails.
    It may seem out of place
    But they do it in case
They bump into the Princess of Wales!
JOHN DINAN

A gentleman player of squash,
Preferred to appear rather posh.
    When the ball hit his eye
    Instead of a cry
Or a curse, he politely said, 'Gosh'.
            PENNY WATSON

A talented sportsman named Hugh,
Remarked – 'Of the games I pursue,
    I find it is snooker
    That's loaded with lucre.
If you're needing advice, take my cue!'
                  NOEL A. JONES

A snooker professional of rank,
After fluking the black, was quite frank;
    He said, 'I'm distraught
    At the fame it has brought'.
And he cried all the way to the bank.
                  F. HORNER

A cross-channel swimmer called Meaker,
Near Calais got cramp and grew weaker;
    When a shark known as 'Jaws'
    Came and ripped off his drawers
And created the first channel streaker!
          MICHAEL CLAUGHTON

Said a cross-channel swimmer named Jim:
'Though the exercise keeps me in trim,
    The ferry's much quicker
    And duty-free liquor
Don't half weigh you down when you swim!'
          JOHN DINAN

At the poolside they each strike their poses
Graceful arm-lines and straight pointing toeses
    But the swimming in sync
    Must produce quite a stink
Or else why have the pegs on their noses?
GILLIAN FIELDING

An inveterate bachelor named Denis,
Never trusted mixed singles at tennis;
  Just before the first ball
  Called the umpire, 'Love all,'
So he fled, screaming, 'Feminine menace'.
VICTOR BALHAM

We're all sick of the flashy misdeeds,
Of the tennis stars, mainly top-seeds;
  They're so spoilt and so rich
  It's a pleasure to switch
Our allegiance to well-behaved Swedes.
RICHARD WATTS

A Wimbledon star of ability,
Used a certain crude verbal facility,
　To broadcast his grudges
　Against the line judges
And speak of the umpire's senility.
F. HORNER

Martina Navratalova,
Wins Wimbledon over and over;
But is she a he
In search of a she
Or has she a transvestite chauffeur?

MONICA RIBON

There was a young lady called Carling,
At Wimbledon was such a darling.
　　With her partner named Mabel
　　She quaffed her Black Label
And flew over the net like a starling.
J. BATSFORD

A problem John McEnroe's got:
To be nice to the linesmen or not?
　　Will cursing them all
　　Change the bounce of the ball
Or help them see things that are not?
FIONA BAILE

Two Tahitian girls whose hibiscus,
Slipped while they were throwing the discus,
    Enquired of the judge
    Who checked them for drugs,
'Is this an excuse, Sir, to frisk us?'
                     ANNE ROLLINGS

There was a young chap from Gibraltar,
Who practised to be a pole-vaulter.
    Someone let off a squib
    And, no word of a fib,
He vaulted right over to Malta.
                    MRS P. ROBERTS

With support from the pipes and the tabor,
The MacInnes let fly with his caber;
    His arm was awry
    He endangered West Skye,
And put paid to the croft of a neighbour.
                    BOB LOVELESS

When Volleyball's played in the West,
It's a game very much like the rest;
    When it's played in the East
    It becomes a rare feast
Of devilish gusto and zest.

                  BOB LOVELESS

There are two types of yachtsmen; the cruising
And the racing (who can't abide losing);
    But what both types adore
    Is coming ashore
For the serious business of boozing.

JACK DALGLISH

The floggers of gaspers had found,
That 'the box' was worth many a pound.
   But the Beeb said, 'We fear
   Yer can't do that there 'ere –
Though yer can plug 'em all round the ground'.
REGINALD SPINK

  As the Commonwealth Games are in sight,
The authorities are in a plight;
   For on both track and field
   They're reluctant to yield
That the issues aren't just black and white.
TONY HOARE